totally tara
an olympic journey

totally tara
an olympic journey

tara lipinski

ORIGINAL PHOTOGRAPHY: SIMON BRUTY

WITH TEXT BY MARK ZEIGLER   UNIVERSE

"it felt so perfect..."

February 20, 1998: It was raining in Nagano, Japan, when Tara arrived at White Ring arena. She was in second place after the previous day's short program. Tara was one of the last to skate, and as she waited at a neighboring rink, she was told by coach Richard Callaghan only that Michelle had "skated well." Michelle had, in fact, skated a clean, elegant program, and most had predicted that Kwan's mistake-free performance would be enough to win gold. But Callaghan wasn't worried: "She loves to come from behind," he said.

The music began, and for four minutes Tara mesmerized an audience of millions with a powerful combination of elegance and energy. While Kwan was skating not to lose the gold medal, Tara went on the ice to *win* it. It had been said that having Tara one place behind you is like having a fighter jet on your tail. Indeed, Tara won so emphatically at Nagano that journalists described the free skate as a "take-no-prisoners" competition; others said that Tara didn't win the medal, she "ripped it away."

But in the end, it was a victory forged not only by four minutes of perfection on the ice, not only by a lifetime of dedication, but most of all by a very pure love of the sport. As Tara explained a day later: "Last night I wanted to win, but I didn't want to win so badly that it messed up my performance. I went out there and I tried to do it for the love of skating. I think that's why my program came out so well."

When it came time for the medal ceremony, Tara embraced the moment as if she had lived it many times before, loving it more each time. She seemed to know just what to do. Then again, she had been practicing the ceremony since she was two—when she climbed atop an overturned tupperware container and motioned to her mother for a length of ribbon and some flowers so she could mimic a medal ceremony on TV during the 1984 Summer Games. "I was so happy standing there," Tara told reporters after the Nagano medal ceremony, "but maybe a little sad knowing I was going to have to get off eventually. It just felt so good and so perfect."

"I wanted to capture her love of skating and her very, very pure Olympic ideal."

—Choreographer Sandra Bezic, fall, 1997, describing the long program she and Tara had designed for Nagano.

HUGGING COACH RICHARD CALLAGHAN IN THE KISS-AND-CRY AREA MOMENTS AFTER THE VICTORIOUS LONG PROGRAM. FOUR MINUTES EARLIER, JUST BEFORE SHE PUSHED ONTO THE ICE, RICHARD HAD LEANED OVER THE BOARDS AND TOLD HER, "YOU'VE HAD A GREAT TWO WEEKS HERE. YOU'VE HAD FUN. YOU'VE TRAINED HARD. NOW JUST GO OUT AND FINISH THE EXPERIENCE."

introduction

by Mark Zeigler

Fourteen-year-old Tara Lipinski was the last person to skate the long program at the 1997 United States Figure Skating Championships in Nashville, Tennessee. Her performance would decide the ladies' singles title, and Tara was nervous.

Moments earlier, Michelle Kwan, the reigning world champion, had skated her long program, which had been far from flawless. It was Tara's turn now, and she thought back to the 1996 World Championships, ten months earlier. Tara had skated her short program there immediately after Japan's Midori Ito. Ito's performance had been mediocre, and the jolt of seeing the ice humble a skating legend had then unnerved Lipinski. Tara had faltered, falling repeatedly and finishing the night buried in 23rd place. Now, in Nashville, Tara found herself once again following a skating favorite who had fallen.

RELISHING THE 1997 WORLD CHAMPIONSHIP VICTORY. PHOTO © DUOMO/PAUL J. SUTTON.

There were 16,052 people in the sold-out
Nashville Arena, with ABC television cameras
broadcasting the event to millions of Americans.
Tara recalled the previous year and vowed not to
let it happen again. She gritted her teeth and
pushed onto the ice.

Four minutes and seven triple jumps later, Tara
Lipinski was the youngest United States senior
figure skating champion in history. Peggy Fleming
was fifteen years, six months old when she won
her first senior national title in 1964. Sonya
Klopfer had been fifteen years, one month in
1951. Tara was fourteen years, eight months old.
"I'm in shock, but it's great," Tara told
reporters afterward. "I can tell you right now,
I'm soooo on a different wavelength." She was 4
feet, 8 inches tall. She weighed 78 pounds. A
week earlier she had lost her last baby tooth.

The skating world was in shock—it just shouldn't
have been. Yet Tara had been doing this all her
life—gliding across uncharted waters . . . or
ice, rather. She was standing at six months. She
was running at one year, riding a little bicycle
at two. At three, she took up roller skating; at
five, she won a regional championship.

When Tara was six, a friend's mother suggested to
Pat Lipinski that her daughter try skating with
blades instead of wheels. Pat and Jack took Tara
to the ice-skating rink . . . and winced. "She
was falling around," Jack remembers. Pat and Jack
went to the snack bar to get a cup of hot choco-
late. When they returned, Tara was not falling
around anymore. She had translated everything
she learned from roller skating onto the ice.
She was a natural.

To this day, a photo hangs in the Lipinskis'
living room of that first day on the ice. It
serves a dual purpose—a reminder of how far

12

PERFORMING A LAYBACK SPIN IN THE SHORT PROGRAM AT 1997 WORLDS. PHOTO © DUOMO/PAUL J. SUTTON.

Tara has come and a testament to her boundless talent. Just down the street is the Detroit Skating Club, her practice rink in the Detroit suburb of Bloomfield Hills, Michigan. It was there, one morning about a month before the 1997 Nationals, that coach Richard Callaghan decided to challenge Tara and increase the difficulty of the combination jump in her long program. Instead of a triple Salchow-triple loop jump combination, Callaghan suggested she try a triple loop-triple loop, a combination landed in competition only once by a man and never by a woman. To pull off a triple loop-triple loop, which requires two consecutive takeoffs and landings from the same foot, a skater must flawlessly land the first jump in order to execute the second. Tara, who is particularly strong on edge jumps, nodded and skated out from the boards. She landed it on her first try.

Less than three years earlier, Tara was not even on the initial roster for the 1994 Olympic Festival in St. Louis, a mini-Olympics for American athletes. She was an alternate. A spot opened at the last moment, and she flew to St. Louis—where she won, of course. She was twelve years, three weeks old. That broke the previous record for the youngest gold medalist at a sports festival, an honor held until then by gymnast Shannon Miller.

The following winter she finished third in her first National Championships at the senior level and qualified for the World Championships, in Canada. After her disastrous short program, she wowed the Canadian crowd with a sparkling long program and moved up eight spots. The secret was out. The little girl who grew up in Sewell, New Jersey, could skate. Shortly after the competition in Canada, new rules were passed that prohibited skaters from competing

ON THE PODIUM AT THE 1997 WORLD CHAMPIONSHIPS. PHOTO © DUOMO/STEVEN SUTTON.

at the World Championship competition if they had not turned fifteen by the previous July. Tara would be only fourteen come 1997 Worlds. American skating officials lobbied for her to be "grandfathered" into the competition. The following year she was the youngest U.S. champion in history. Two months after that, she replaced Norway's legendary Sonja Henie as the youngest world champion ever.

About this time, a reporter from *Texas Monthly* magazine asked her how it all happened so quickly. Tara paused to consider the question. "I really don't know the answer," she said. "All I can say is that I kept practicing."

Indeed, for all the apparent ease and grace with which Tara glides across the ice, radiating her unique blend of charm and elegance, the life she has chosen is one of extremely hard work. For years, it was eating dinner on a tray table in the back seat of the car while riding home from practice over the Delaware Bridge. It was waking up at 3 A.M. after the family's move to Texas to get ice time at the local shopping mall's rink. It was having to dodge a Christmas tree in the middle of the rink during the holidays.

LEFT: PERFORMING A CAMEL SPIN IN THE LONG PROGRAM AT THE 1997 WORLD CHAMPIONSHIPS. MIDDLE: EMBRACING SILVER MEDALIST MICHELLE KWAN ON THE PODIUM AT 1997 WORLDS, AS THE USA GOES 1–2. RIGHT: GLIDING TO VICTORY NEAR THE END OF THE LONG PROGRAM AT 1997 WORLDS. PHOTOS © DUOMO/STEVE SUTTON (LEFT) AND DUOMO/CHRIS COLE (MIDDLE AND RIGHT).

Tara's family has made sacrifices, too: moving to the East Coast and then the Midwest in order to train with the nation's top coaches while Tara's father, an executive at an energy company, stayed in Texas to work. The family also had to refinance their house and take out loans to pay skating bills (once she moved to the elite facility in Detroit, expenses started exceeding $50,000 per year).

Amazingly—despite all the sacrifices and the grueling schedule—Tara manages to make time for a good deal more than skating. Pat Lipinski will be the first to say that Tara has no shortage of friends and fun: "Socially, Tara's unbelievable. I seem to have fifteen kids at the house every other day." In fact, all the hard work seems to come naturally to Tara: "Everyone's going to pick on the bad things, but just know that I do all this to skate," Tara once said. "My mom doesn't push me. My coach doesn't push me. It's my thing. . . . It's my skating, and I just want you to know that I love it and this is the best I can be."

For Tara, carving a path to the Olympic Games was not solely the product of hard work, talent, and determination; it is also a story of faith. Faith in oneself and the faith to reach for a dream, no matter how distant it may seem along the way. Every day, Tara wears around her neck a rose medallion representing St. Thérèse of Lisieux, "The Little Flower"; Tara also makes the nine-day novena prayer with her mother before competitions. The medallion was given to her by the mother superior of an orphanage in Corpus Christi, Texas, and its presence reminds Tara and her family that she has to lift her eyes from the ice from time to time, to look heavenward to find the strength of spirit that no amount of training can provide.

REACHING FOR HER DREAM: A BEAUTIFUL EXTENSION, 1997 SKATE AMERICA EXHIBITION. FOLLOWING PAGES: A CANDLE FOR ST. THÉRÈSE, NOTRE DAME CATHEDRAL, PARIS.

ch.1

86327

it began
with a rainbow

For Tara, the choice of music and the choreography of her programs tell a very distinct story—a dream, really—one that is deeply personal and inspirational. For her long program, she skated to a song called "Rainbow":

"The rainbow is my dreams and everything that I want to come true—the Olympics, winning, everything. In the beginning of the program, I'm dreaming of it. The hard part, all the technical things, is like me running uphill to find the rainbow. Then I get up there and it's raining. In one part, I'm doing my footwork and it's like I'm dancing in the rain. All of a sudden, as the music slows, I see the rainbow, I've beaten the storm, and I see my dream. At the end, it's finally mine."

Sandra Bezic, Tara's choreographer for the long program, helps Tara express her story on the ice:

"Tara's programs are about honesty, about celebrating the realities and challenges of her life. They are meant to portray what Tara is and who she is. When you're fifteen, you're filled with changes. Sometimes you're a child and sometimes you're a woman. Tara skates like a woman. She jumps like a woman. Her dreams are vivid and self-motivated and determined, but they're also pure and ideal in a beautifully childlike way. In her Olympic program, her dream is a vision of a rainbow, and of her struggling through the rain to reach that vision."

REHEARSING "THE RAINBOW"; SETTING UP FOR A LUTZ. **FOLLOWING PAGES:** TARA IN A PRACTICE DRESS WORKING ON LAYBACK AND SIT SPINS FOR HER LONG PROGRAM.

landing the program

begin with a song...

The competitive figure-skating season generally begins in
the fall and runs through the following spring, but, for
Tara, preparation began the summer before with the long,
painstaking process of choosing the right music for her
programs: "It was the end of the summer, and I just couldn't
find anything. I'd get a piece and say, 'Let's see if I
can skate to it,' but I just didn't have the feeling."

Tara enlisted the help of choreographer Sandra Bezic, a
former Canadian pairs champion who has worked with Brian
Boitano, Kurt Browning, Katarina Witt, Kristi Yamaguchi,
Lu Chen, and the Stars on Ice tour. "If Tara doesn't feel
the music, there is no sense taking it to the ice," Sandra
said. "We went through every musical piece, listening to
CD after CD, just waiting for Tara's eyes to light up and
say, 'This is the one.'"

Tara first heard the soundtrack from the movie *Anastasia*
during a coming attractions preview. Upon being told that
the soundtrack wasn't available yet, she was granted an
advance screening and was immediately captivated by the
story of the Russian princess. For her short program, Tara
ultimately settled on instrumentals from two songs in the
movie: "Journey to the Past" and "Once upon a December."
"I sort of identify with Anastasia," Tara said, "How she
looks back in her past to her home life. I look back to
my home in New Jersey where I grew up, to my Uncle Phil,
and to everything that inspired me to skate." Tara's short
program is also very much about the courage to face the
present. "*Courage* is the word," Sandra Bezic said of the
program. "Tara is a fifteen-year-old girl facing very
adult fears."

Landing on the music for the long program was less of an
ordeal, since there is more time and fewer compulsory
moves to consider. Tara and Sandra's priority was finding
music that allowed Tara maximum freedom of expression. For
her long program, Tara chose "Scenes of Summer" by Lee
Holdridge, along with "Rainbow" by Carl Davis, a composi-
tion Scott Hamilton called "grand and Olympian."

choreographing a sound program...

Once Tara and Sandra had landed on the right music,
the mechanics of choreography were clinical at first:
the main concerns being pacing, learning the music, and
mapping out the compulsory moves. It is generally
accepted that a top skater can sustain full speed on
the ice for about 90 seconds during a program; therefore, controlling speed, conserving energy, and creating "rest periods" in between physically exhausting
jumps and spins is crucial. It is also crucial that
the skater is totally confident that the program allows
for landing every required jump before applying the
emotional nuances. This is, in effect, the challenge
faced by the choreographer: to elegantly combine equal
parts artistry and athleticism.

All this has to be done with a very keen ear to the
music and the timing it imposes. In the long program,
for example, Sandra and Tara edited "Rainbow" until
they found they were up to a minute short, prompting
Tara to choose an excerpt from "Scenes of Summer" to
fill the remaining minute. Sandra then worked with the
skater to create a program that follows the music's
inherent movements, highlights, and pauses.

It took ten days, working in two-hour stretches at a
time, to put together Tara's basic sequences. According
to Sandra, it is essential to concentrate first on the
mechanics, including daringly difficult jumps close to
the end of the program, and then on the finer points
of expression. Tara may be physically small, light, and
quick, but she tends to prefer sweeping movements and
longer phrases of music that allow her to glide into
her jumps, which are also very fast and smooth.
Sandra's choreography focuses on these characteristics
to insure that every single movement, from a jump to
the sweep of an arm, has meaning, that every element
in the program helps to "tell a story," with a beginning, a middle, and a crescendo for an ending.

For Sandra, skating is a very public spectacle, so telling a skater's story with honesty, both physically and emotionally, is essential for a successful performance. Her job is to search for ways to communicate, through the art of skating, whatever truths and inspirations are driving the skater. In fact, the choreographer must encourage the skater to reach for the limits of her personal potential, without regard to comparisons with other skaters.

Sandra's goal was to support the young world champion as she moved to an even higher level. As Sandra keenly observed: "Tara's Olympic programs are a real milestone for her. Tara has an aura now when she steps on the ice. She holds herself like a champion. She wears the crown on the ice, and is comfortable with that role. She has that confidence and maturity. Her vocabulary has increased on the ice. . . ."

A PRACTICE SESSION WITH CHOREOGRAPHER SANDRA BEZIC. PHOTOS COURTESY DINO RICCI/SANDINO PRODUCTIONS.

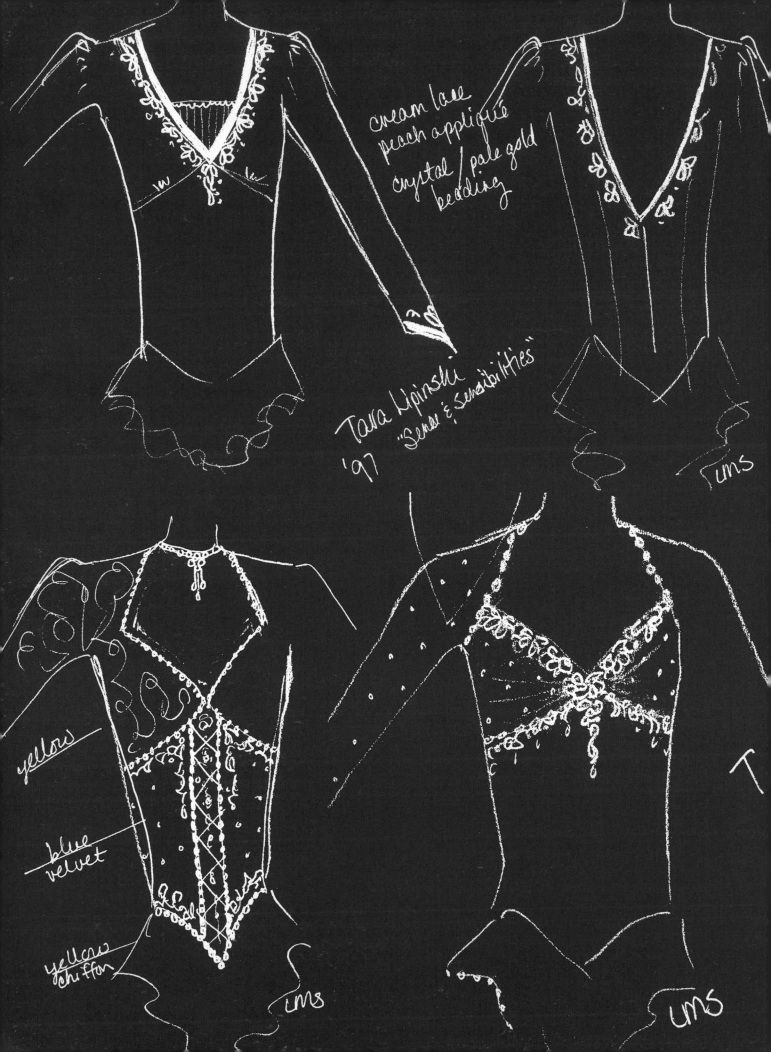

cream lace
peach appliqué
crystal / pale gold
beading

Tara Lipinski
'97 "Sense & Sensibilities"

yellow

blue
velvet

yellow
chiffon

dressing it all up

Tara has one hard and fast rule about her costumes: "No orange." There are a few other no-no's: no sleeveless dresses, no puffy sleeves, no dangles, and not too many sparkles—"I'm not the glitter queen," she has protested.

The real challenge for designer Lauren Sheehan—herself a former figure skater—was creating a perfectly fitting, finely tuned outfit without ever seeing Tara try it on. With the exception of the first long program outfit for the 1997–1998 season, which the Lipinskis decided to change, there was never a fitting for any of Tara's costumes. Because of this, Tara and Lauren developed a unique, long-distance dialogue concerning all aspects of her costume: color, material, weight—every detail. Tara, who is informed and decisive about fashion, needed to describe in detail what she envisioned so Lauren could interpret Tara's vision.

Before settling on a backless blue dress for the long program, Lauren had originally crafted a blue dress with a rainbow-colored top. Initially, Tara wanted the dress to be plain, but ultimately, she gave in to the addition of a few beads and sequins to highlight the outfit. The dress for the short program displayed detailing that evoked the Russian themes of *Anastasia*. Both dresses represented an important step in Tara's on-ice transition from girl to woman, as they were far more sophisticated than the previous "pony-tail-and-floppy-skirt" outfits worn during her early years.

TOP: LAUREN SHEEHAN'S DESIGNS FOR TARA'S "SENSE AND SENSIBILITY" ROUTINE FOR THE 1997 WORLD CHAMPIONSHIPS. BOTTOM LEFT: THE FINAL DESIGN FOR "ANASTASIA." BOTTOM RIGHT: THE FINAL DESIGN FOR THE OLYMPIC GAMES LONG PROGRAM DRESS. FOLLOWING PAGE: TARA'S BOOTS ARE CUSTOM-MADE HARLICKS. FOR TARA, LIGHT ON HER FEET, A PAIR OF BOOTS GENERALLY LASTS FROM EIGHT TO TEN MONTHS.

"The love of the sport, that really comes through.
Tara doesn't look like anyone is making her do it.
It's coming from within. And that's important."

—Christy Ness
coach of Kristi Yamaguchi

ch.3

ballet and artistry

ONE OF THE DAILY SESSIONS WITH MARINA SHEFFER IN THE BALLET ROOM AT THE DETROIT SKATING CLUB. FOR TARA, BALLET HELPS REFINE "THE LINE, THE WAY YOU STROKE ON THE ICE."

on artistry

Tara has been taking ballet and non-classical dance coaching to support her skating since age seven. Now, she builds her artistry and presentation skills through daily ballet instruction with her Russian ballet coach, Marina Sheffer. As Tara puts it, ballet helps a skater master how to "make it all look easy." For Marina, coaching a skater in balletic movement and artistry poses some unique challenges:

> Like dancers for the theater, every skater must be an actor, must express a world of emotion without a word. With skaters, it's even more difficult, because they have to compress this expression into just a few minutes—and without a supporting cast. The most important goal is to inspire emotion in the audience, to inspire them to feel involved in what's happening on the ice.

Much of Marina's work with Tara occurs at the rink, where Tara can apply the principles she learns from Marina. The two also work routinely in the studio, where Tara can use the mirror to focus on subtle elements like facial expression and hand movements. When Marina first began working with Tara, in the summer of 1996, much of the focus was on cleaning up Tara's lines and working on proper extensions. A year later, Tara, who would practice at home until her arms ached, had improved her presentation so dramatically that Marina was able to focus on these more detailed elements of artistic expression.

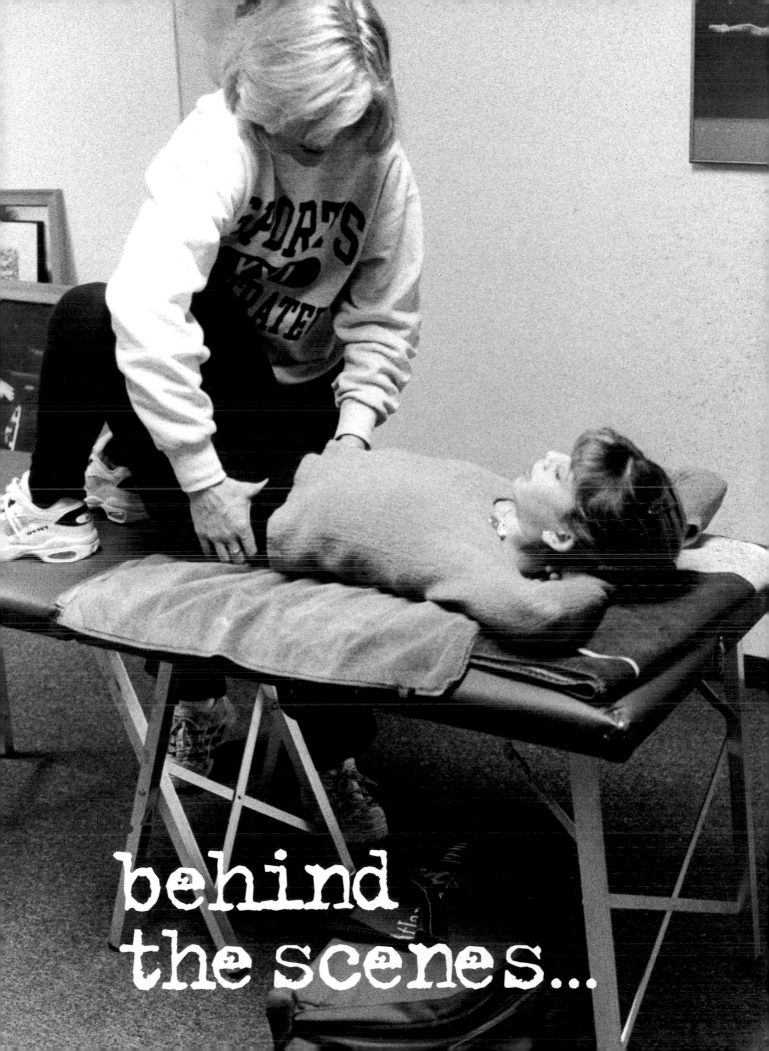

behind
the scenes...

grace, poise and a lot of sweat...

Tara's training schedule is, to put it simply, grueling. A normal day starts with about 45 minutes of stretching and physical conditioning with trainer Britta Altabani, then no fewer than four 45-minute sessions on the the ice, plus another session with Marina Sheffer. And after that? Four hours of schoolwork with three tutors.

Each on-ice practice session depends on what elements coach Richard Callaghan thinks need the most work. A typical morning session starts with a slow warmup with just a few jumps, followed by a basic run-through of the short program. Then there is usually some focused work on individual elements — footwork, say, or a particular jump sequence — followed by an actual full run-through of the program with music. Tara will sometimes experiment with different musical selections during practice. The afternoon sessions are usually devoted to the long program.

In the practice rink Tara has a reputation for being a die-hard perfectionist. She just isn't comfortable unless she's run through her program at least four times in a day. And if she misses a jump, she will simply not leave the ice until she's landed it.

TARA STRETCHING WITH HER PHYSICAL TRAINER, BRITTA ALTABANI. BRITTA IS A USOC-CERTIFIED SPORTS PHYSICIAN WHO ACCOMPANIED THE U.S. SNOWBOARDING TEAM TO NAGANO. ON THE WALL OUTSIDE THE TRAINING ROOM HANGS A PICTURE OF MIGGS DEAN, WHO REPRESENTED THE DETROIT SKATING CLUB IN WORLD COMPETITIONS IN THE LATE 1950S.

7:00 A.M.
Wake up, breakfast

tara's
typical day

8:15 A.M.
Stretch, warm up (with Tara
here are pairs champions
Punsalan and Swallow)

9:15 A.M.
On ice: first
45-minute session

10:15 A.M.
On ice: second
45-minute session

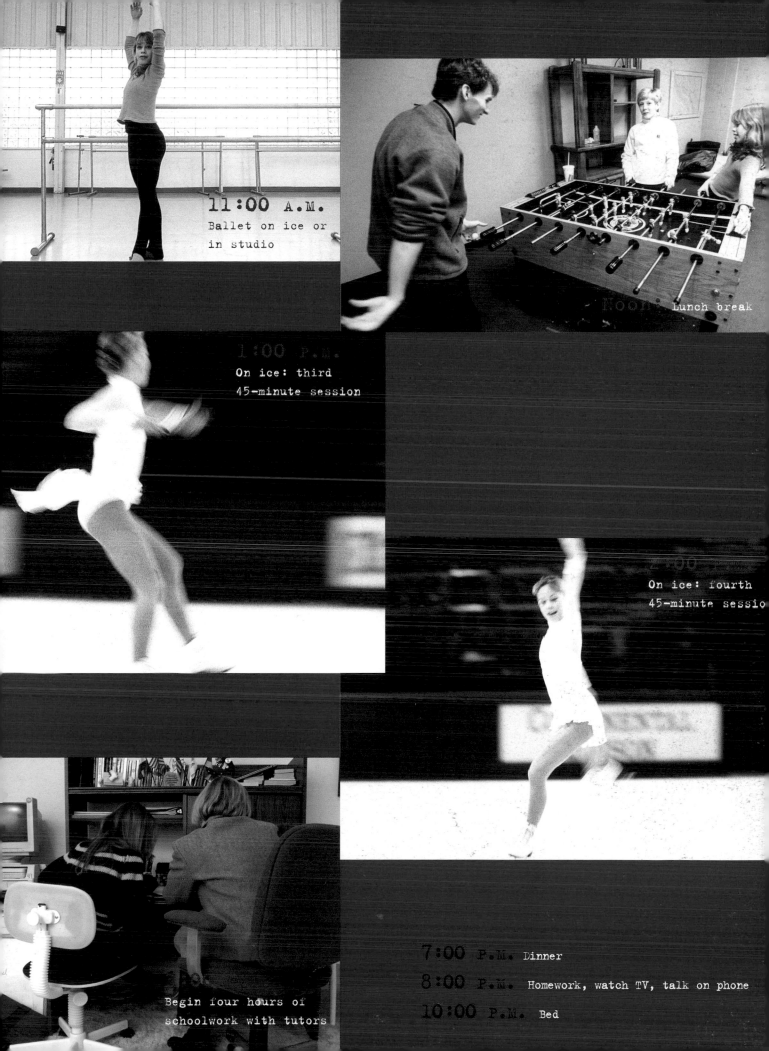

11:00 A.M.
Ballet on ice or
in studio

Noon: Lunch break

1:00 P.M.
On ice: third
45-minute session

On ice: fourth
45-minute session

Begin four hours of
schoolwork with tutors

7:00 P.M. Dinner

8:00 P.M. Homework, watch TV, talk on phone

10:00 P.M. Bed

He's not "Richard." He's not "Coach." He is, simply,
"Mr. Callaghan." When asked why she refers to her
coach as if he were her grade school math teacher,
Tara just laughs, saying that's just the way it's
always been.

MR. CALLAGHAN

Richard has been instrumental in helping Tara make
the delicate transition from girl to woman—which is
hard enough without millions of people watching.
Fortunately, "Mr. Callaghan" has a bit of experience
in handling massive talent in very young packages: he
has coached Todd Eldredge since he was a toddler and
was also the coach of Nicole Bobek when she captured
the National Championship title in 1995.

There are only about four or five coaches in the
country considered capable of developing an Olympic
champion, which led Tara to Richard. She was also
attracted to the Detroit Skating Club, a massive
three-rink facility that can properly accommodate
nationally qualified skaters. Normally, Tara shares
the ice with only about four other skaters—including
Todd Eldredge, Erin Pearl, Suzanna Szwed, and Erin
Sutton. Tara also depends on assistant coach, Craig
Maurizi, who helps Tara daily with the finer points
of jumping and technique, and Megan Faulkner, Tara's
childhood coach and longtime friend and confidant.

Richard can be a conservative coach and doesn't take
unnecessary risks (for a long time, he would not let
Todd Eldredge attempt the quadruple jump in competition). He therefore seemed to be a perfect match for
Tara during her journey to the Olympic Games: her
always pushing forward, his tugging ever so slightly
on the reins. Richard's original plan was to make
the U.S. Olympic team and have a "respectable" plac-
ing at the 1998 Winter Games at Nagano, positioning
Tara to go for it all in 2002 on home soil in Salt
Lake City. The night Tara won Nationals in 1997,
however, Callaghan reconsidered his plan. . . .

"She's so focused to skate. Her attitude is always,
'If that's what I have to do to be the best,
that's what I'll do.' Tara won't leave the ice
until she feels complete."

—Erin Elbe

ABOVE: PAT SAYING GOODBYE TO TARA BEFORE LEAVING TO RUN AN ERRAND. TARA HAS ANOTHER TWO SESSIONS TO SKATE. OPPOSITE: TAKING A BREATHER AT A PRACTICE SESSION IN DETROIT. THE DETROIT SKATING CLUB IS DEDICATED ENTIRELY TO FIGURE SKATING; IT BOASTS ONE OLYMPIC-SIZED AND TWO U.S.—SIZED RINKS AND A COMPETITIVE ROSTER THAT IS SECOND TO NONE. ITS MEMBERS WON FIVE OF TWELVE POSSIBLE MEDALS IN THE MAJOR NATIONAL COMPETITIONS LEADING UP TO THE 1998 OLYMPICS.

"I don't have to be perfect, but I need to be comfortable. Practicing is hard, but there's a sense of accomplishing something, something I'm good at. Every day I try a little harder; that's what I try to express through my program. But skating is definitely more fun than hard work."

"That's just the kind of person she is, the kind of skater she is: to come back twice as strong after something goes wrong. If she misses something, she goes back and does it over and over and over. She knows you have to fight for everything you get in this sport."

—Todd Eldredge

ch. 5

competition

te america, trophée lalique,

champion series final

skate america
(October 1997, Detroit, Michigan)

At Skate America, the sport returned to the scene
of its biggest crime. On a snowy day in January
1994, Nancy Kerrigan was injured by an assailant at
this event, launching the Kerrigan-Harding scandal.
Now, however, there was a rivalry of a different
sort. A friendly rivalry. Lipinski vs. Kwan . . .
Tara vs. Michelle.

All eyes were turned on Tara after her unforgettable
victories at the beginning of 1997 during Nationals
and Worlds. So after a summer and early fall of
intense preparation, the first major pre-Olympic
figure skating competition arrived with incredible
fanfare—and unprecedented pressure. . . .

Each had won a World Championship, Kwan as a fifteen-year-old in 1996 and Tara as a fourteen-year-
old in 1997. This was their first meeting of the
new season. Because of the summer Tom Collins tour,
Tara had a late start preparing for the long season, and this was the first time she had to put her
challenging new programs to the test in a major
competition. Tara captured second place.

OPPOSITE: TWO RIVALS WARM UP AT SKATE AMERICA. PAGES 66–67: AN ON-SITE PRACTICE SESSION AT SKATE AMERICA.
RICHARD USUALLY TELLS TARA JUST BEFORE SHE COMPETES: "GO DO YOUR WORK." PAGES 68–69: TARA GETTING SOME
LAST-MINUTE ADVICE FROM RICHARD BEFORE SKATING HER SHORT PROGRAM AT SKATE AMERICA, WHILE MICHELLE KWAN
FACES THE PRESS. PREVIOUS PAGES: EXHIBITION PERFORMANCE AT SKATE AMERICA.

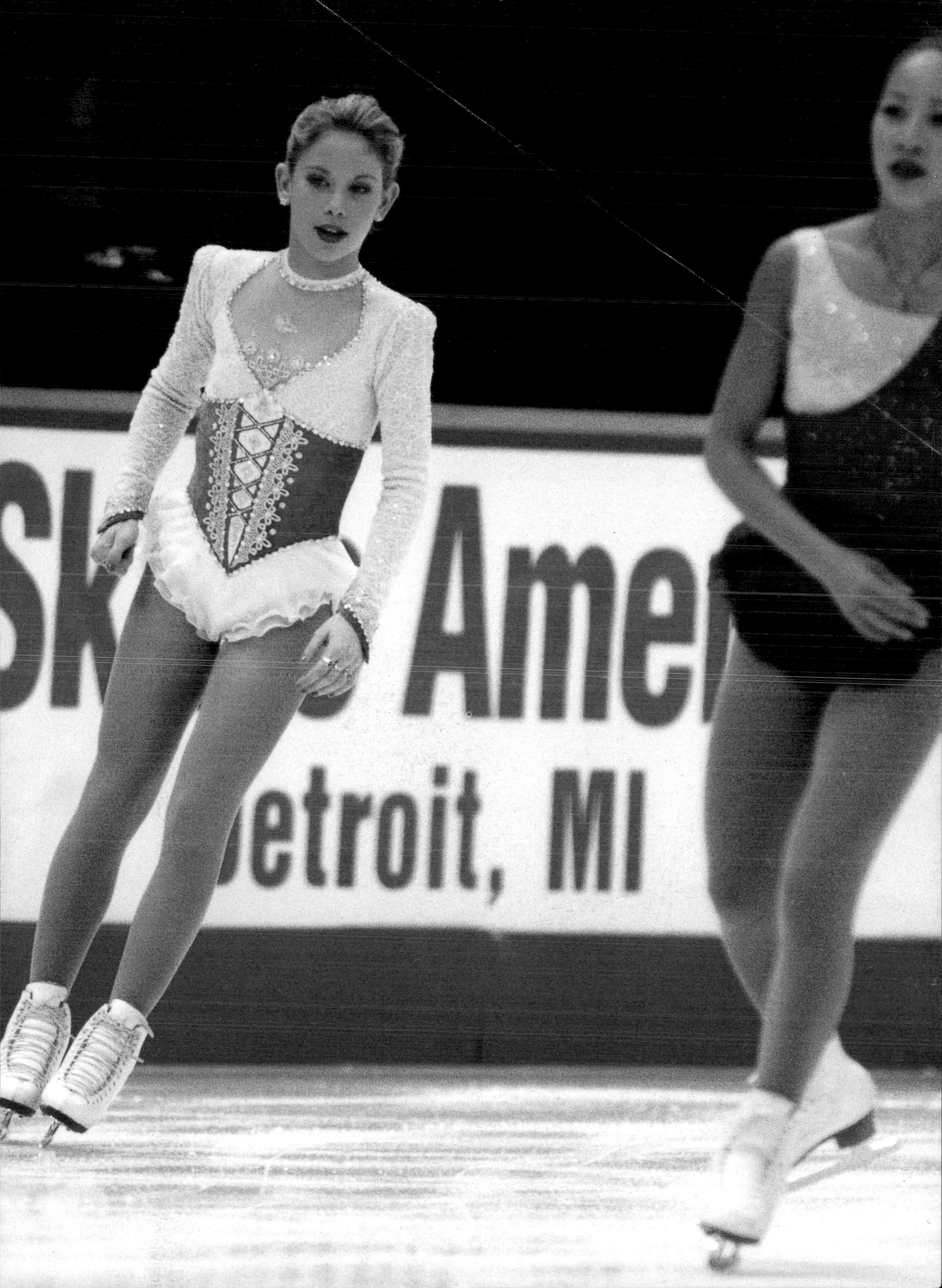
etroit, MI

Tara went into the season's second major senior-level competition with a bad cold, facing a competitor's hometown crowd. Tara's short program was excellent. In the long program, she ended up doubling two of her planned triple jumps, but she matched France's Laetitia Hubert for triples in the final count. In the judges' tally, Tara finished second to Hubert, a former world junior champion.

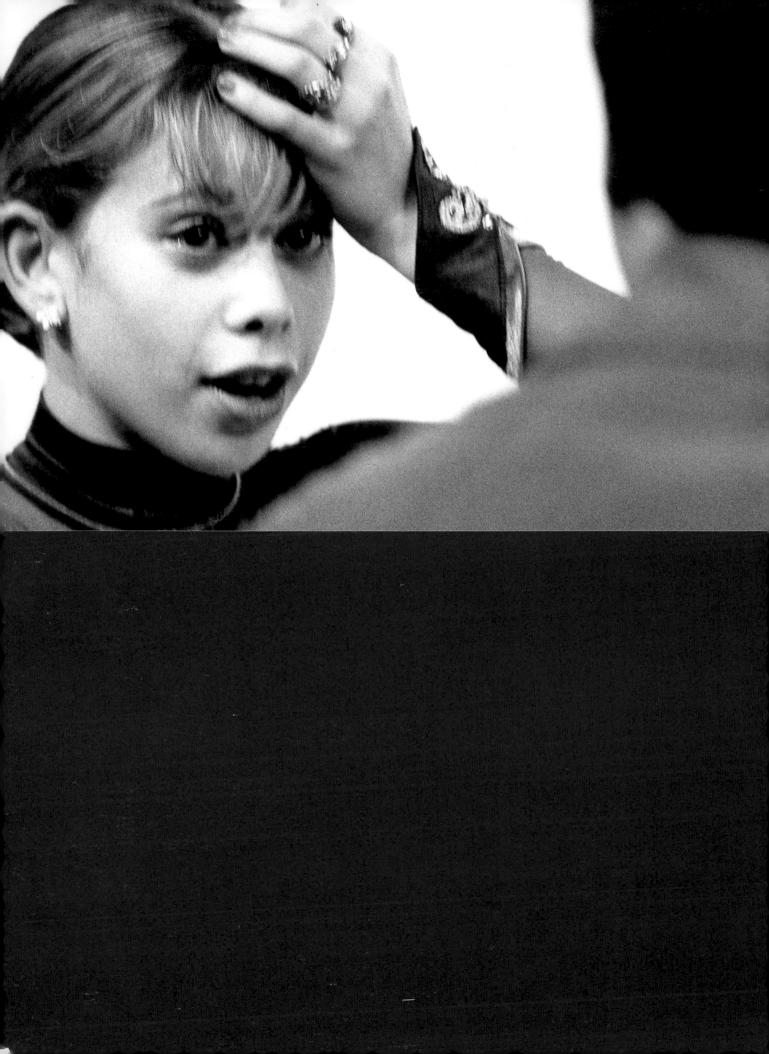

anatomy of the short program
2½ TERRIFYING MINUTES

In competitive figure skating, the short program counts for one-third of a skater's total score, but as one sportwriter has pointed out, "it accounts for two-thirds of the nerves." There are eight required elements in the short program—from which a skater can select a number of moves that fit the bill—and they can be performed in any order. It can last for no more than 2 minutes, 40 seconds.

Tara's short program:

1. Layback spin
2. Spiral sequence
3. Triple Lutz/double loop
4. Flying camel
5. Footwork into a triple flip jump
6. Double Axel jump
7. Footwork
8. Combination spin

BELOW: TALKING WITH RICHARD CALLAGHAN AND MEGAN FAULKNER AT A PARIS PRACTICE SESSION. MEGAN HAS BEEN COACHING TARA SINCE AGE NINE AND ACCOMPANIES TARA TO EVERY COMPETITION, PROVIDING VALUED MORAL SUPPORT. **OPPOSITE:** TARA WEARS HER 1997 WORLD CHAMPIONSHIP RING ON HER LEFT INDEX FINGER; THE OTHER RINGS ARE FAMILY HEIRLOOMS.

THIS EXHIBITION SKATE IN FLORENCE, SOUTH CAROLINA, OFFERED A WELCOME PAUSE IN THE STRING OF INTENSE 1997–1998 COMPETITIONS.
TARA SKATED TO "REACH," BY GLORIA ESTEFAN. HER SHOW PROGRAMS ARE CHOREOGRAPHED BY SUSIE WYNNE.

champion series final
(December 1997, Munich, Germany)

This was the first time Tara entered a major competition as
defending champion. She responded like a veteran, winning both
the short and long programs with a cool efficiency belying her
years. Germany's Tanja Szewczenko skated immediately before Tara
and treated the home crowd to the performance of her life. As the
flowers and applause rained down, Callaghan told Tara: "Hey, pre-
tend we're back at C rink, and it's just you and me working."
Tara did, landing seven triple jumps and receiving a slew of 5.9s
from the judges. Even the German judge rated her long program the
best of the evening. "It was so emotional for me because I finally
skated better," she told reporters. "I felt like I really defend-
ed my title. I'm just so happy. This is going to be the best
Christmas." With the Munich medal in her hands, Tara had medaled
in every major competition of the season, a solid follow-up to
her remarkable "triple crown" of the 1996-1997 season.

TARA TURNING IN ONE OF HER FINEST PERFORMANCES EVER AT THE CHAMPION SERIES FINAL IN MUNICH. PHOTOS © TEMPSPORT/DMITRI IUNDT.

waiting in the wings

Before competitions, Tara does her own makeup and hair: "When I first went on tour, I saw all the makeup these kids had. I just went home and bought everything. I learned how to use it and picked up tips from everybody. And whenever I do photo shoots, the makeup artists always give me tips. I try to make it look natural, not too yucky."

Tara absorbs herself in the details: "I try not to think about competing or the other competitors. If I skate clean, there's nothing else I can do."

For every event, she packs her favorite, well worn skate bag with skates, new laces, a stuffed animal or two, a blue glass charm and good luck key ring, plus two competition dresses, two back-ups, and an extra pair of blades.

competition mode

The days, hours, and minutes before a competition involve
intense preparation, both mental and physical. Tara, her
mother, and often a friend or two of Tara's usually arrive a
few days early and rest up for the competition practice sessions. For Pat, it's important that Tara is able to bring a
friend along to competitions: "Other moms look at me like, What
are you doing? Their kids have to sit in the room and not talk
and not play. But I know that Tara, believe it or not, really
goes to these things to enjoy herself." During these on-site
sessions, Richard Callaghan will often ask Tara, without warn-
ing, for what he calls an "on-command performance": a complete
run-through of her program, skated as if she were really at the
competition. This helps Tara enter what her parents call "competition mode." Tara has one pre-competition ritual that she says
is more important than all the others, however. She and her
mother usually visit a children's hospital the week of a big
event. "It brings us back to reality. You really begin to think
that life revolves around landing a triple Lutz. You forget
there is a world out there, and people are living and dying."

a few words from mom

Just outside the spotlight at virtually every event Tara's ever done is Tara's mother, Pat Lipinski. And back in Sugar Land, Texas, taking care of the five dogs and making sure the skating bills get paid, is Tara's father, Jack. Do Pat and Jack push their daughter to skate? On the contrary. . . Pat explains:

"You can have a firm hand when they're little, but when they're teenagers there's no way at this level that a kid's going to do it unless they want it very badly. I think it's tragic when a skater's really not skating for herself. For us, it's not a family business. If we all went back to normal again, that would please Jack and me tremendously. We've often wanted to. Tara knows that. Not having the pressure from us to perform, I think that's been very helpful to her. It's like being in a sport and being free."

ABOVE AND RIGHT: TARA WITH MOM BEFORE A SHOW. PAT WOULD NEVER BE ALLOWED NEAR THE LOCKER ROOM BEFORE A COMPETITION, MUCH LESS COCO, TARA'S DOG. PREVIOUS PAGES: A COMFORTING PRE-COMPETITION MOMENT WITH COCO, HER FAVORITE "GOOD-LUCK CHARM." COCO (TARA'S FRIEND ERIN NAMED HER PUPPY FROM THE SAME LITTER "CHANEL") ACCOMPANIES TARA TO VIRTUALLY EVERY EVENT, BUT WAS NOT ALLOWED TO GO TO NAGANO BECAUSE OF QUARANTINE RESTRICTIONS.

on nerves

Jack Lipinski says the hardest part is not being able to help Tara when she's on the ice: "When I'm at competitions, I usually say goodbye to Tara in her room, give her a kiss and tell her to skate great, then duck out of sight. I try to find a place to sit where Tara can't see me — the thought of distracting her even for a second is terrible. Pat used to pace up and down while I watched, but now we both end up pacing back and forth until it's over. I just can't wait until it's over."

Pat Lipinski admits she doesn't fare much better: "You don't want to be around me when she's skating in competition."

And Tara herself: "I do get nervous. I get really nervous out there. But then I just think, 'I want to do this.' I think about the times I've skated so well under pressure and I try to remember what that felt like. . . . Trust yourself. That's the most important thing for me to remember, definitely."

"Boy has Tara paid her dues. People don't realize how long she has been skating. You could say that since she's taken her first breath she's felt as though she's been on skates, because that's all she remembers."

— Pat Lipinski

HEADING HOME: TARA WITH "UNCLE" PHIL CALLAHAN (PAT'S COUSIN AND CLOSE FAMILY FRIEND).

ch.7

off the ice

downtime

A veteran world traveler at fifteen, Tara still has a domestic
side. She likes to bake, especially desserts: Jack says she
makes a mean ice-cream sundae. She also likes to do needlepoint
and cross-stitch. Books on her recent reading list include *Gone
with the Wind*, the book and movie from which her mother got her
name. Tara is also a faithful viewer of the TV series
"Friends," and die-hard "Wheel of Fortune" addict. In fact, one
of her dreams is to one day appear as a contestant on that
show. By her own account, Tara's home life isn't all that different from that of most girls her age: "I do normal things
when I'm off the ice. I relax, I call my friends, go to the
mall, go to the movies—you know, normal things."

Tara also admits to another big habit: shopping. Clothes and
makeup usually top the list. What type of clothes does she shop
for? "Anything, any season. I love starting over for a new season. I'm tired of shopping for winter. Every winter, I wish
summer would come so I could start shopping for it." Tara is
adamant about choosing her own clothes and doing her own
makeup—for leisure and competition.

Tara, however, is a competitor at heart, and one of her off-
the-ice passions is foos-ball, the longtime American rec-room
favorite. At her rink in Detroit, Tara, Todd Eldredge, and the
other skaters have set up a mini-tournament that keeps them
busy between training sessions. Todd has held the "foos-ball
world champion" title for some time, but Tara has victory in
her sights: "When I'm playing anything I think, 'I want to
win.' I get a little disappointed when I don't win." Indeed,
she's got Todd on the defensive: "She doesn't like to lose,
even at foos-ball. I always beat her, but she's destined
to beat me."

Tara's downtime is more than baking, TV, and foos-ball, of
course. She is enrolled at the River Oaks Academy in Houston
and is tutored each night. One of the toughest dilemmas for her
family was deciding to stop attending school full-time after
fifth grade. Her tenth-grade curriculum included Spanish,
English lit., math, and physical science. Like her father, who
has a law degree, Tara sees herself in law school eventually.

MAKING A BAGEL AS COCO WATCHES INTENTLY. DOES TARA HAVE ANY SPECIAL DIET PREFERENCES? "YEAH. SEEFOOD. SEE FOOD AND EAT IT,"
SAYS HER FATHER.

ABOVE: KILLING TIME ON THE TOUR BUS WITH ERIN ELBE, MICHELLE KWAN, AND BRIAN BOITANO, SUMMER 1997. PAT: "THAT KID JUST FINDS SOME WAY TO ENJOY HERSELF WHEREVER SHE GOES." PHOTO © DAVE BLACK. **OPPOSITE:** IN THE DRIVER'S SEAT, PUTTING HER LEARNER'S PERMIT TO GOOD USE. **PREVIOUS PAGES:** A FOOS-BALL TOURNAMENT IN PROGRESS, WITH TODD ELDREDGE AND VICTORIA MASON. **FOLLOWING PAGES:** A NIGHTLY TUTORING SESSION WITH SPANISH TUTOR LINDA MICHAELS IN TARA'S "UPSTAIRS CLASSROOM" AT HOME IN MICHIGAN.

"I can do it! I can do it!"

—Tara (at the wheel)

it's always a party

Tara has always taken a friend with her to each of the past three National Championships. Pat stays in one room, and Tara stays in another with her friend. Pat Lipinski doesn't seem to mind:

> I don't ever want to say about Tara, "She didn't have a life." She's told me, "Mom, if I can't have it this way I don't want it," and that's fine. Most of the time, she thinks of skating as one big party. I have never seen anything like it before. She just astounds me. I think it was something that even her coach had to get used to. Here's this kid, and it's always like she's going to a party. She's been like this ever since she was a baby. Her birthday parties had to have thirty-five kids, and for sleepovers, never fewer than fifteen. I have the pictures to prove it. She just likes tons of people. She's always got to have a friend.

Pat remembers that right before the Olympic Games Richard Callaghan had cleared the other skaters off the ice for Tara and Todd's practice sessions. But Tara and Pat, accustomed to a rink alive with other skaters, went to the nearby mall for a few hours, "just to be around lots of people, to feel 'normal.'"

PREVIOUS PAGES: TODD GIVES TARA A LIFT. OPPOSITE: TARA IN HER HOTEL ROOM AT 1998 NATIONALS, ON THE PHONE WITH HER FATHER, JACK. LATER, TARA AND LINDSEY WATCH INTENTLY AS ERIN ELBE GETS ON THE PHONE TO "MAKE PLANS," ACCORDING TO PAT. BEFORE THEY FELL ASLEEP AFTER TARA'S COMEBACK AT NATIONALS, ROOMMATE AND BEST FRIEND ERIN REMEMBERS TARA WHISPERING TO HERSELF—PROBABLY THE FIRST TIME SHE ALLOWED HERSELF TO DO SO—"I'M REALLY GOING. I'M REALLY GOING TO THE OLYMPICS." FOLLOWING PAGES: BEAUTY IN THE DETAILS—TARA USED TO COPE WITH NERVES BY BITING HER NAILS, BUT NOW SHE'S MORE LIKELY TO GET THEM MANICURED. AT THE U.S. NATIONALS, SHE AND HER FRIENDS, LINDSEY WEBER, ERIN ELBE, AND VICTORIA MASON, EACH TAKE THEIR TURN AT THE HOTEL SALON.

a friend indeed

On the Tom Collins tour in the summer of 1997, Tara would watch reigning Olympic gold medalist Oksana Baiul skate every night, learning from her example. Back in 1994, at Lillehammer, a six-teen-year-old Oksana skated a breathtaking, remarkably sophis-ticated program, edging out Nancy Kerrigan for the gold medal. On tour, while rehearsing choreography, Tara would often follow Oksana's lead, listening carefully to her critiques. As Pat noticed: "Tara loved it. She'd sit and listen to Oksana every night—about what was good, what could be improved. It was very helpful to Tara."

OPPOSITE: SEPARATED AT BIRTH? PAT SAYS, "PEOPLE KEEP TELLING ME THAT TARA AND OKSANA LOOK ALIKE." **FOLLOWING PAGES:** WITH ANGELA NIKUDINOV AT 1998 NATIONALS. ANGELA AND TARA HANG OUT A LOT AT COMPETITIONS.

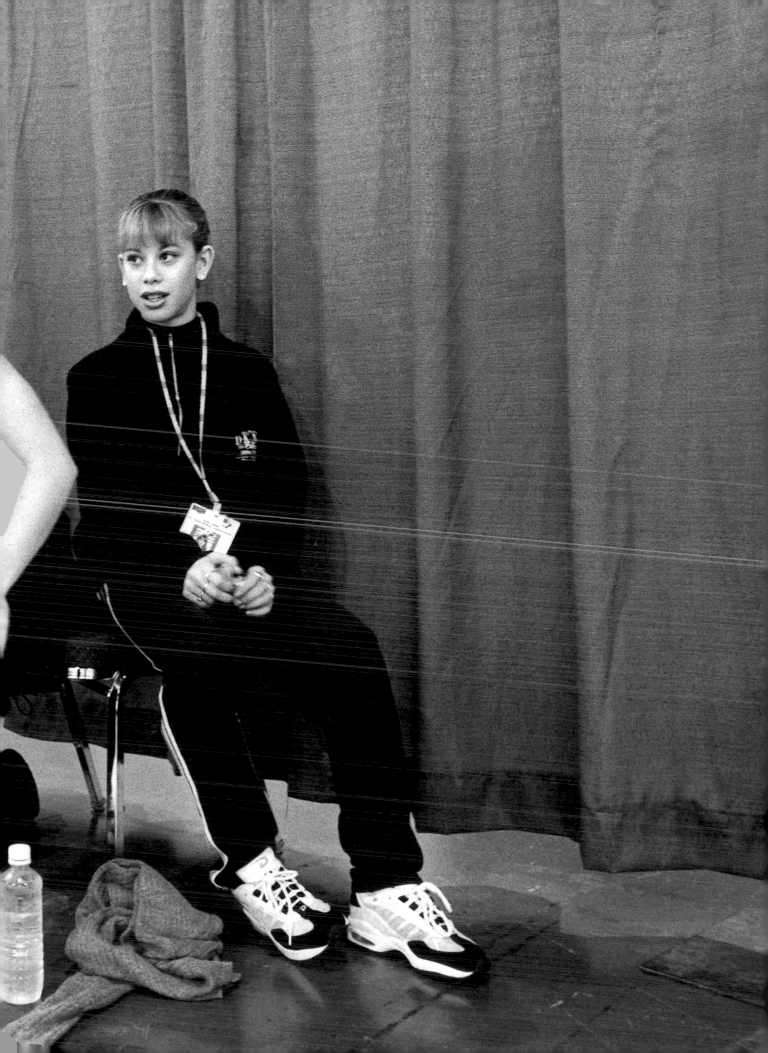

ch.9
en garde:
U.S. nationals '98

perfect redemption

U.S. Nationals, Philadelphia, January 1998: Tara fell on the triple flip jump in the short program and dropped to fourth place, leaving her with only a remote chance at defending her title and automatically qualifying for the Olympic team. Jack Lipinksi remembers the moment: "Totally unexpected. In the weeks leading up to Nationals, she had been skating better than I had ever seen her."

"She has to go home, watch TV, calm down, get a good sleep and she'll be fine," Richard Callaghan said that night. "I gotta say, I think she'll come back and skate great." The next day at practice, Callaghan had her warm up and then immediately try a jump: a triple flip. She landed it cleanly, broke into her trademark smile, and everything in her world was right again. Later that day, a reporter was playing the what-if game with Richard, wondering what if Tara stayed in fourth place after Saturday night's long program. Callaghan answered the question before it could be completed: "She won't be. She's too much of a fighter."

Was Tara nervous going into the free skate? Pat: "You could see the fear in her eyes. I could see it before the long program. She was scared. No matter how many people we had talk to her, it didn't matter. In her mind, she had to make the cut to go to the Olympics." Prophetic words. Tara took to the ice Saturday night and landed seven triple jumps, including the difficult triple loop-triple loop combination. She hurdled over Nicole Bobek and Tonia Kwiatkowski into second place overall. "For me, I knew it was a fluke, just a silly mistake," Tara said of her short program. "Tonight I just tried to block out everything and think only about what I wanted to do out there. You know, you have to forget about what you did before and just move on." She was now officially on her way to Nagano, Japan.

PREVIOUS PAGES AND OPPOSITE: THE CLIMAX OF THE LONG PROGRAM AT 1998 NATIONALS. PHOTO THIS PAGE © ALLSPORT/JAMIE SQUIRE. PAGES 114–115: TARA IS METICULOUS ABOUT NOT LETTING HER BARE BLADES TOUCH ANY HARD SURFACE OFF THE ICE; THE SKATE GUARDS COME OFF ONE AT A TIME JUST AS SHE SLIDES ONTO THE ICE AND GO BACK ON THE SAME WAY BEFORE SHE LEAVES IT.

anatomy of the long program:
some room for expression

It was Tara's long program that clinched her comeback. The free skate, or long program, lasts 4 minutes for ladies and counts for two-thirds of the final score. There are no required elements, allowing for more freedom, but generally the top skaters will attempt six or seven triples, including at least one combination jump. A winning long program will also include a series of spins and steps. The marquee feature of Tara's long program was her triple loop-triple loop combination. Also, ending her program with a difficult jump sequence—at a moment when many skaters are rubber-kneed and exhausted—is testament to Tara's strength. In all, Tara had seven triple jumps of five different types planned for her long program.

Key elements in Tara's long program

1. Layback spin
2. Double Axel jump
3. Triple flip jump
4. Triple Lutz-double toe loop combination jump
5. Combination spin
6. Footwork
7. Triple loop-triple loop combination jump
8. Camel to back camel to catch spin combination
9. Triple Lutz jump
10. Spiral sequence
11. Triple toe/half loop/triple Salchow jumps
12. Flying camel to illusion spin combination

TARA SKATING TO AN UNFORGETTABLE COMEBACK IN THE FREE SKATE. "SHE'S NEVER LET HERSELF FALL TWICE IN A ROW IN COMPETITION," SAYS ERIN ELBE. **FOLLOWING PAGES:** AFTER HER STUNNING LONG PROGRAM AT THE 1998 U.S. NATIONALS. TARA DONATES MOST OF THE STUFFED ANIMALS LAVISHED UPON HER DURING PERFORMANCES TO THE PAX CHRISTI ORPHANAGE IN CORPUS CHRISTI, TEXAS. **PAGES 124-125:** FACING REPORTERS BEFORE COMPETING IN PHILADELPHIA

"That's one of my strong points, I think, to look at a bad situation and come back strong from it, to prove to people that I can do something."

ch:10

public
performance

"In skating you have to act as an adult. You have to be careful. I'll be with my friend Erin at Nationals and we'll be hysterical in the elevator and then all of a sudden we come to a floor and say, 'OK, shhhh, don't laugh.'"

—Tara

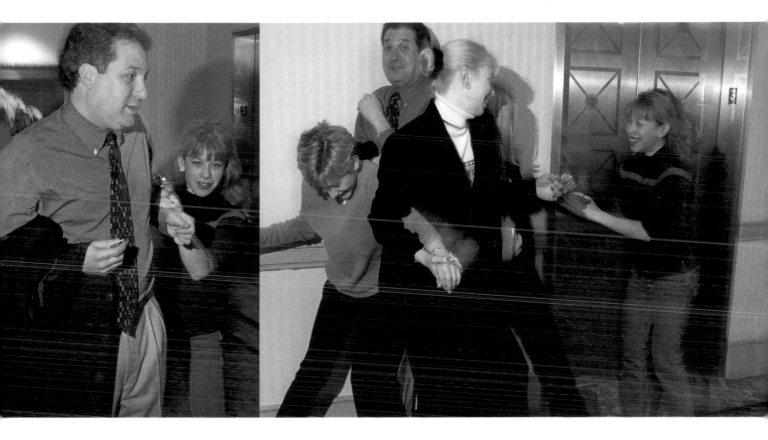

"It's funny. You take her outside that arena, out of the spotlight, as quick as thirty seconds after she's done skating, and it's Tara again, the same girl who grew up around the corner and who we took to dinner. When she puts the skates on, she's the best in the world. When she takes the skates off, she's just our Tara."

—"Uncle" Phil Callahan

OPPOSITE: DKNY PROMOTIONAL APPEARANCE IN NEW YORK. PREVIOUS PAGES: TARA IN PARIS SHOOTING A FOX-TV SPECIAL. ABOVE: "BEATING UP" TARA'S AGENT, MIKE BURG. FOLLOWING PAGES: PAT WARMING TARA'S FEET AFTER A PROMOTIONAL SKATE IN NEW YORK'S CENTRAL PARK. PAT: "THAT WAS THE SICKEST SHE'S EVER BEEN. SHE HAD A 104.2-DEGREE FEVER THAT NIGHT." PAT AND MIKE BURG WANTED TO CANCEL, BUT THIS WAS A COMMITMENT TARA REALLY WANTED TO KEEP, BECAUSE LOTS OF CHILDREN WERE WAITING TO SEE HER SKATE. "TARA JUST LOVES KIDS," PAT EXPLAINED, "AND THE COMMITMENT TO PERFORM FOR THEM WAS SOMETHING TARA WANTED TO HONOR."

WITH NEW YORK CITY SCHOOL KIDS IN CENTRAL PARK.

an olympic experience

Unlike many of the high-profile skaters at the XVIII
Winter Olympic Games in Nagano, Tara had opted to stay
in a shared room at the Olympic Village, literally
surrounding herself with other athletes and with the
intense energy of the Games. But the night before each
performance, she had decided to seek some much-needed
peace and quiet in her parents' hotel room. The day of
the long program, Tara said goodbye to Mom and Dad,
closed the door behind her, and headed for White Ring
Arena.

A few moments later, as Jack and Pat tell it, there was
a light knock at the door. Tara leaned into the room
and said, simply and without hesitation, "I'm gonna do
it." This has become a sort of pre-skate ritual for
Tara: leaving for the competition and then returning
with a few final, prophetic words. This time, however,
Pat seemed to notice something different in Tara's
voice. That same afternoon, Tara had been unusually
quiet during dinner; she had leaned over her plate of
spaghetti and whispered to her mother: "I think I'm
scared, Mom." Now, in the hotel room, the fear was
gone, replaced with confidence and determination.

Indeed, everything about those two weeks in Japan was
different. Tara had come to Nagano with more on her
mind than taking home a medal. She came to the Games to
fulfill a larger dream, to absorb and welcome this event
that she had previously experienced only on television.
Tara had not come all the way to Nagano just to curl up
in an athletic cocoon and await six-and-a-half minutes
of competition. As Tara put it: "I wouldn't want to
come to this competition and stay in a hotel. I'm so
glad I got to meet all the other athletes and have fun,
rather than just skate. If you don't do well, you don't
want that to be your only experience."

Then again, Tara's best defense against pre-competition
nerves has always been to surround herself with people,
and she did just that at Nagano. She ate at the athletes' cafeteria. She posed for a photo with a 516-pound

WITH AMERICAN ATHLETES AT THE OPENING CERMONIES AT NAGANO. TARA: "I HAD BEEN TRYING TO IMAGINE WHAT THE OLYMPICS
WOULD BE LIKE, AND IT'S BETTER THAN I THOUGHT."

sumo wrestler named Akebono and with speed skaters and cross-country skiers. She had her nails done at the beauty counter, made Olympic patches in the sewing room, shared McDonald's with Nicole Bobek in her room (which she adorned with stuffed animals), read fan e-mail at the IBM Surf Shak, attended sporting events with her teammates, hung an American flag in her window, and even walked around in an endless search for Canadian hockey player Eric Lindros (she had a brief encounter with another hockey player after winning the gold: Wayne Gretzky approached her in the athletes' cafeteria and went away with her autograph). She was miked by CBS to narrate the opening ceremonies, and later, after her victory, she visited the children's ward at a local hospital.

In the end, it was this passion for the Olympic experience that infused Tara's skating on that fateful Friday evening. "Once the music came on," Tara said, "I knew I was at the Olympics and what the Olympics were about, and everything just came together." Tara's longtime coach, Megan Faulkner, who was with Tara during all her Olympic practice sessions and at both competitions, could see this inspiration the moment Tara stepped on the ice: "From her first practice, from the first moment she stepped onto the rink here, she embraced the Olympic experience. She thought, 'I might never experience this again. I'm doing the Olympics and I'm doing the Olympics the way I want to do it.' And that came through in her skating."

That night, after the medal ceremony, after the tearful long-distance phone calls, and clamorous press interviews, Tara finally climbed into bed at around three in the morning and sank into such a deep sleep that Megan Faulkner was able to curl Tara's hair for an early-morning television appearance without waking her. In the wee hours, a moderate earthquake shook central Japan, shaking most people from their beds. The next morning a reporter asked Tara what she though about the quake. "What earthquake?" she said. Tara hadn't even noticed, she figures she had slept right through it, her gold medal snugly around her neck.

CLOCKWISE FROM TOP RIGHT: WITH USA ATHLETES AFTER HER VICTORY; VISITING A SHRINE IN NAGANO; WITH MOM AND A HANDFUL OF GOLD; OUTSIDE WHITE RING ARENA; THE OLYMPIC FLAME; WITH MICHELLE KWAN DURING A CBS POST-COMPETITION INTERVIEW; COMPARING MEDALS WITH A USA WOMEN'S HOCKEY TEAMMEMBER; TARA AND DAD IN HER ROOM; A VERY HAPPY FAMILY; MUGGING FOR THE CAMERA WITH, FROM TOP, NICOLE BOBEK, TIPPER GORE, MARY LOU RETTON, AND TENLEY ALBRIGHT (FIRST U.S. WOMAN SKATER TO WIN A GOLD MEDAL). FOLLOWING PAGES: FACE TO FACE WITH MICHELLE KWAN AS THEY APPROACH THE PODIUM. ONE HEADLINE IN U.S. PAPER THE NEXT DAY READ, "KWAN SKATED ON THE ICE; LIPINSKI FLEW BEYOND IT." PHOTOS COURTESY JACK LIPINSKI.